COLORING BOOKS SWATCHES

This color chart book was created to help you choose the right color every time.
By adding your group of colors to a chart you can quickly see which color is right for the project you are working on.

Simple coloring in the sample square and write the pencil's color and product name beside it.
When your Group Chart is done, add the name of the Group Chart along with its page number in the handy index located at the front.

There a few ways you can utilize these charts.
You can organize your charts by type product. You can add the colors from your favorite box of colored pencil to one set of charts and then add the brand of colored pencil in another set of charts.
Or, you can all of the same color to one set of charts. Imagine all your reds in one place. All your blue in one chart set for quick comparison.

As with all paper products, when adding makers to the charts, it is suggested that you slip a waterproof barrier behind the sheet so it doesn't leak through to the next chart behind it. Household waxed paper or cling plastic works well for this purpose.

One more thing ...
You can also create sets of companion colors for instant reference.
That gorgeous turquoise beside that gleaming lime green. Just draw a diagonal line across the square and color in the two matching colors, jot down the names. It's ready for me the next time you want to use that winning combination.

I hope you enjoy organizing your colored pencils with this Color Chart book as much as I do.
Sharpen your pencils! GO!

Happy Coloring!

~ Kay D Johnson

Enjoying this book?
Please leave me a review. I would love to hear your feedback.
Thank you for your support. Your purchase is greatly appreciated.

Group Name	Medium	Page #

Group Name	Medium	Page #

Group Name	Medium	Page #

Group Name	Medium	Page #

Group Name	Medium	Page #

Group Name	Medium	Page #

Group Name	Medium	Page #

Group Name	Medium	Page #

Group Name	Medium	Page #

Group Name	Medium	Page #

Group Chart:______________________________

...

Group Chart:______________________________

...

Group Chart:______________________________

Group Chart:______________________________

...

Group Chart:______________________________

...

Group Chart:________________________________

...

Group Chart:________________________________

Group Chart:______________________________

...

Group Chart:______________________________

...

Group Chart:______________________________

...

Group Chart:______________________________

Group Chart:______________________________

...

Group Chart:________________________________

Group Chart:________________________________

...

Group Chart:________________________________

...

Group Chart:______________________________

Group Chart:______________________________

...

Group Chart:______________________________

...

Group Chart:________________________________

...

Group Chart:______________________________

Group Chart:______________________________

Group Chart:______________________________

...

Group Chart:______________________________

...

Group Chart:______________________________

...

Group Chart:______________________________

...

Group Chart:___________________________

Group Chart:________________________________

Group Chart:______________________________

...

Group Chart:______________________________

...

Group Chart:______________________________

...

Group Chart:________________________________

Group Chart:____________________________

...

Group Chart:______________________________

...

Group Chart:______________________________

Group Chart:________________________________

Group Chart:______________________________

...

Group Chart:______________________________

Group Chart:_______________________________

Group Chart:______________________________

...

Group Chart:______________________________

Enjoying this book?

Please leave me a review.

I would love to hear your feedback.

Thank you for your support.

Your purchase is greatly appreciated.

www.ingramcontent.com/pod-product-compliance
Lightning Source LLC
Chambersburg PA
CBHW081740220526
45468CB00008B/2182
* 9 7 8 1 7 9 2 6 3 6 8 3 7 *